D0845482

PENS
and
NEEDLES

PENS and

Literary Caricatures by

Selected and Introduced by

NEEDLES

DAVID LEVINE

JOHN UPDIKE

 ANDRE DEUTSCH

FIRST PUBLISHED 1970 BY
ANDRE DEUTSCH LIMITED
105 GREAT RUSSELL STREET
LONDON WC1
COPYRIGHT © 1969 BY DAVID LEVINE
ALL RIGHTS RESERVED
PRINTED IN GREAT BRITAIN BY
LOWE AND BRYDONE (PRINTERS) LTD
LONDON
ISBN 0 233 96160 7

DAVID LEVINE, *par lui-même*

The man above knows what he looks like from the side;
this is extremely rare. Rarer still are caricaturists of his
caliber. Their signature certifies an epoch. In 1963, when
the newly founded *New York Review of Books* began to
publish the drawings of David Levine, the art of caricature in America was quiescent; the theatrical cartoons of
Al Frueh in *The New Yorker* had ceased, Al Hirschfeld
had become primarily a decorator of advertisements,
and William Auerbach-Levy, the most artful of all, had
rounded off his career with an elegant album entitled—
a question he had too often heard—"Is That Me?" These
men had followed the linear tradition of Ralph Barton
and Max Beerbohm; economy was the soul of their wit,
and their mood, as they reduced the features of this or
that celebrity to a cunning black-and-white design, par-
took of the genial mood of showbiz.

Levine, instead, flung himself in a fury of crosshatching upon his subjects. His style looked past Beerbohm to the three-dimensional grotesques of Daumier and Tenniel. No weary pucker or complacent bulge of physiognomy could slip through the supple net of his penstrokes, and every corner of the face—that vulnerable patch between the eyebrows, the unseemly area behind the chin, the mute folds of the ears—was brought into a focus whose keenness transcended the mild demands of "humor." On the gray expanse of the *New York Review* pages his etched homunculi seemed astoundingly *there;* one wanted to pick them up and put them on the shelf. Now, in the form of this book, one can.

Our selection concentrates upon literary figures. Drawn in fortnightly installments to illustrate topical book reviews, the gallery of modern authors approaches completeness. Mann and Borges are missing, and one wonders what Levine would do with Salinger's sad handsomeness or Kierkegaard's bent beauty. But how good it is to know that Gide has no top to his head, and that Truman Capote has no chin, resting, like Baudelaire, within his bowtie like an egg in an eggcup. Levine is not so much an observer as a visionary. Working principally from photographs, he evolves a concept, a monstrous breathing idea. His grasp of this idea deepens with time; of the two versions of Malraux in this volume, the one is a caricature and the other is a caricature of a caricature. Of the three Becketts, the smallest and earliest has the innocence of wit; it puns the man and buzzard. This simile is absorbed and heightened in the alarming metaphor of the profile, with its drastically eroded cheek, its delirious pinpoint eye, its incredible chopping-knife of an ear. And the lava contours and volcanic turtle-neck of the third drawing seem gouged from chaos and quite intimidate any thought of satire. Levine's evolving style (see also the two of Galbraith, the two of Orwell) re-invents the gargoyle, that antidote to the angel and necessary adjunct to a complete humanism. All we humans, beneath the faces that would proclaim for each a separate individuality, share the worse-than-simian weirdness of thinking reeds. Mankind is a riddle it takes the Gothic style to pose.

Since Levine, as clairvoyant, has liberated himself from the physical presence of the subject, the living and the dead are the same to him, and with uncanny authority he conveys, out of fudged old portraits and stylized prints, the essence of the immortals. Take Browning's wonderfully astute, plump, and conceited left hand; or Ben Franklin's cherry-nosed, finger-snapping display of pragmatic pep; or Casanova's evidently numbing virility. The artist discovers a surprising dandyish sneer on the time-softened face of John Milton, and elicits from the noseless bust of Catullus, at the farthest rim of Caricature's reach, the agonized satyr's howl that resounds through imperial Rome. One looks forward to, yet rather dreads, Levine's inevitable cartoon of Jesus. Unless this is already it:

Our artist was born in 1926 in Brooklyn, where he still lives. He has been quoted as describing himself as "a painter supported by a hobby—satirical drawings." As a painter he is representational and has been described, by John Canaday, as "a legitimate anachronism." In his comic art also he displays somewhat anachronistic qualities. Besides offering us the delight of recognition, his drawings comfort us, in an exacerbated and potentially desperate age, with the sense of a watching presence, an eye informed by an intelligence that has not panicked, a comic art ready to encapsulate the latest apparitions of publicity (Twiggy inspires a drawing too lovely to omit) as well as those historical devils who haunt our unease. Levine is one of America's assets. In a confusing time, he bears witness. In a shoddy time, he does good work. Here he is.

John Updike

CONTENTS

The New World

BENJAMIN FRANKLIN

RALPH WALDO EMERSON

EDGAR ALLAN POE

NATHANIEL HAWTHORNE

MARK TWAIN

(with Huckleberry Finn)

MARK TWAIN

STEPHEN CRANE

HENRY JAMES

THEODORE DREISER

SINCLAIR LEWIS

LEWIS *(with Dorothy Thompson)*

H. L. MENCKEN

THEODORE DREISER and H. L. MENCKEN

THOMAS WOLFE

GERTRUDE STEIN

WILLIAM FAULKNER

F. Scott Fitzgerald

F. Scott Fitzgerald and Ernest Hemingway

ERNEST HEMINGWAY

HENRY MILLER

JOHN O'HARA

KATHERINE ANNE PORTER

T. S. ELIOT

ROBERT FROST

MARIANNE MOORE

W. H. Auden

EDMUND WILSON

24

EDMUND WILSON

MARSHALL McLUHAN

26

LIONEL TRILLING

DWIGHT MACDONALD

Arthur M. Schlesinger, Jr.

JOHN KENNETH GALBRAITH

29

MARY MCCARTHY

WILLIAM STYRON

30

JACK KEROUAC

TRUMAN CAPOTE

31

Norman Mailer, Robert Lowell, Dwight Macdonald

ROBERT LOWELL

NORMAN MAILER

NORMAN MAILER

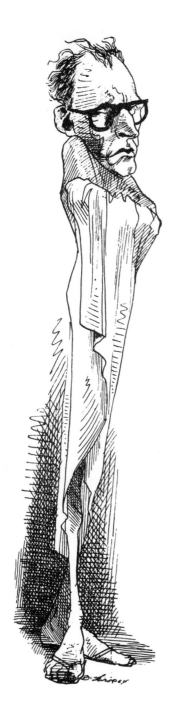

ARTHUR MILLER   TENNESSEE WILLIAMS

EDWARD ALBEE

37

ISAAC BASHEVIS SINGER

BERNARD MALAMUD

38

SAUL BELLOW

VLADIMIR NABOKOV

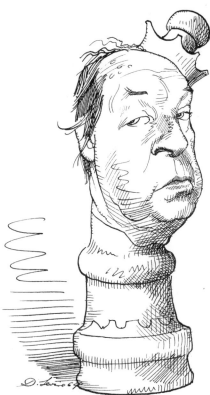

VLADIMIR NABOKOV

SUSAN SONTAG

42

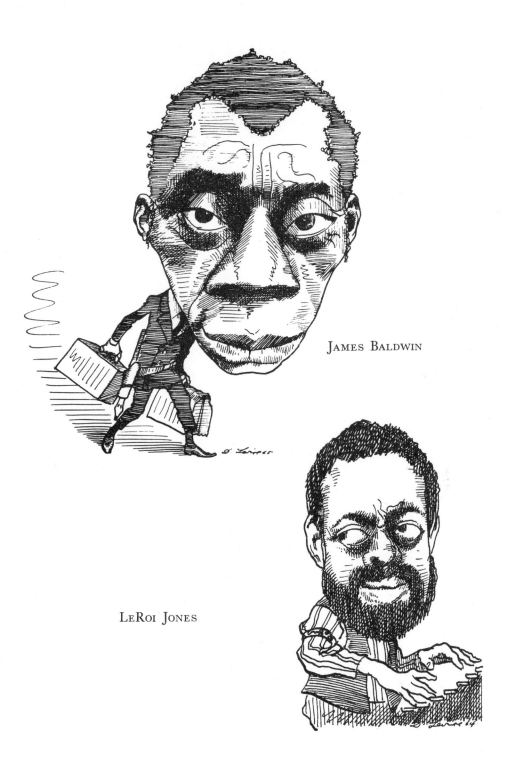

James Baldwin

LeRoi Jones

43

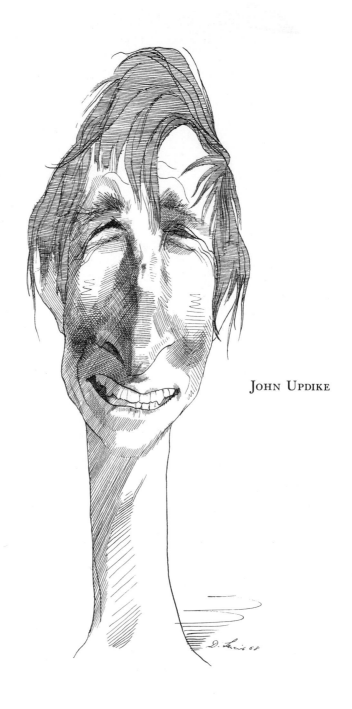

JOHN UPDIKE

PHILIP ROTH

The Continent

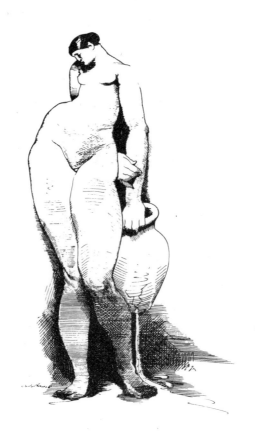

CATULLUS

LEONARDO DA VINCI

BLAISE PASCAL

CASANOVA

51

JEAN BAPTISTE RACINE

The Marquis de Sade

Voltaire

53

Jean Jacques Rousseau

Honoré de Balzac

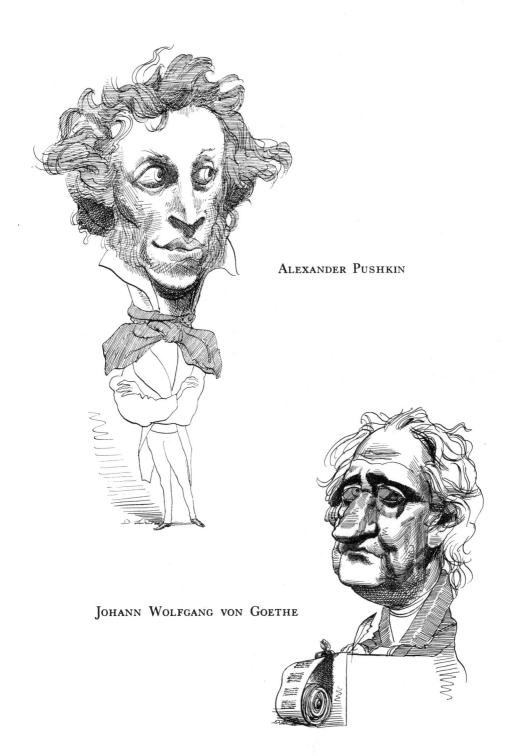

ALEXANDER PUSHKIN

JOHANN WOLFGANG VON GOETHE

55

LEO TOLSTOY

Fyodor Dostoevsky

Anton Chekhov

KARL MARX

KARL MARX *(with Georg Wilhelm Friedrich Hegel)*

HENRIK IBSEN

GUSTAVE FLAUBERT

ARTHUR RIMBAUD

CHARLES BAUDELAIRE

COMTE ROBERT DE MONTESQUIEU

Marcel Proust

JEAN-PAUL SARTRE

SIMONE DE BEAUVOIR

André Gide

ALBERT CAMUS

NATHALIE SARRAUTE

ANDRÉ MALRAUX

COLETTE

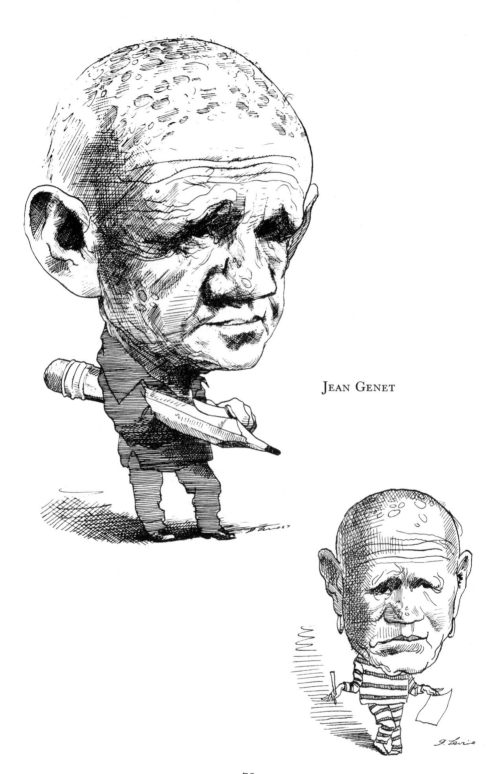

JEAN GENET

LOUIS-FERDINAND CÉLINE

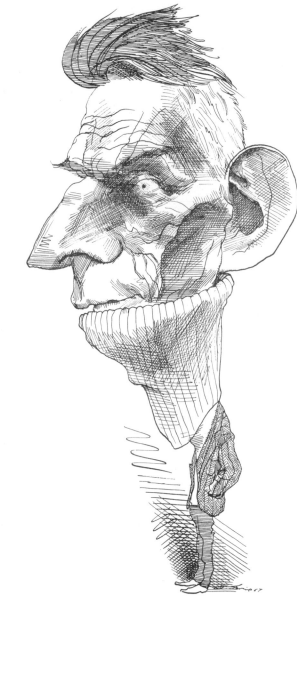

SAMUEL BECKETT

SAMUEL BECKETT

CESARE PAVESE

ALBERTO MORAVIA

ITALO SVEVO

SIGMUND FREUD

RAINER MARIA RILKE

FRANZ KAFKA

KARL JASPERS

78

BERTOLT BRECHT

GÜNTER GRASS

Ludwig Wittgenstein

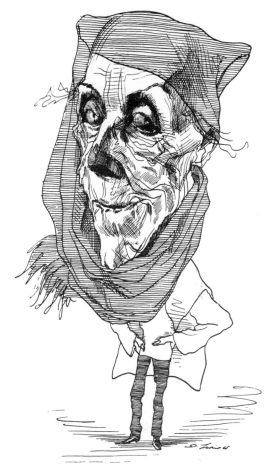

ISAK DINESEN

ARTHUR KOESTLER

81

S. Y. AGNON

Isaac Babel

VLADIMIR MAYAKOVSKY

Maxim Gorky

ILYA EHRENBURG

MIKHAIL SHOLOKHOV

BORIS PASTERNAK

ANDREI VOZNESENSKY

YEVGENY YEVTUSHENKO

ANDREI SINYAVSKY

ALEXANDER SOLZHENITSYN

The British

WILLIAM SHAKESPEARE

FRANCIS BACON

ISAAC NEWTON

97

JOHN MILTON

JONATHAN SWIFT

99

ALEXANDER POPE

EDWARD GIBBON

WILLIAM WORDSWORTH

WILLIAM BLAKE

102

SAMUEL TAYLOR COLERIDGE

LORD BYRON

JOHN KEATS

PERCY BYSSHE SHELLEY

105

ROBERT BROWNING

ALFRED TENNYSON

106

WILLIAM MORRIS

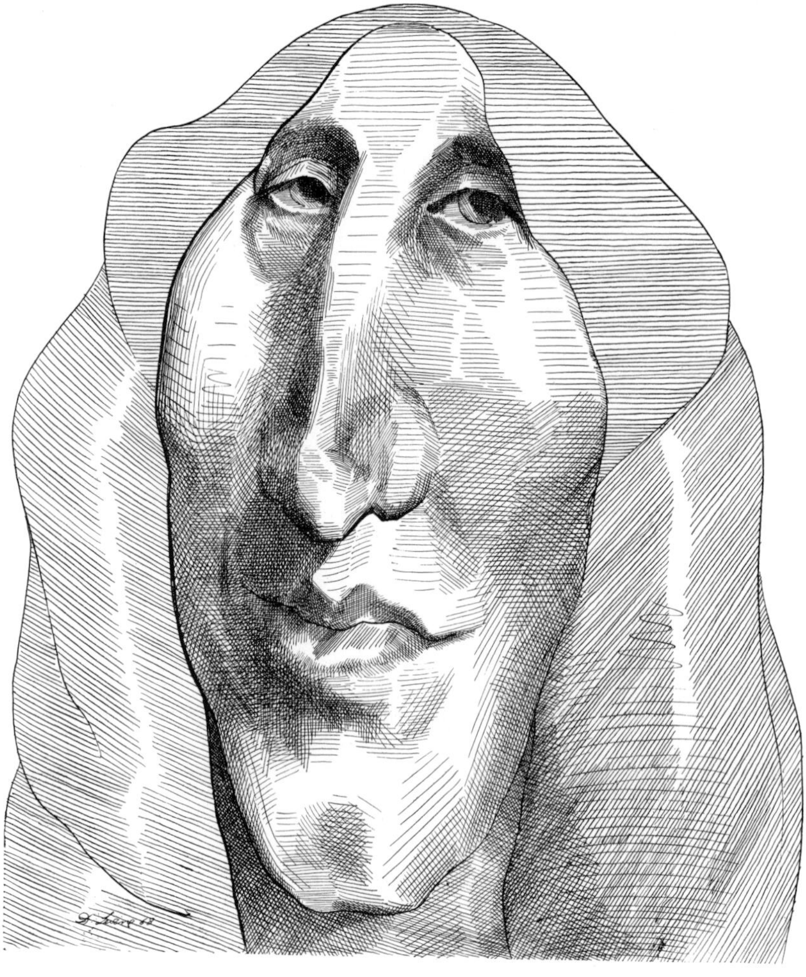

George Eliot

CHARLES DICKENS

THOMAS CARLYLE

CARDINAL JOHN HENRY NEWMAN

More blue, that's it
Turner, now a touch of
naples
that's
it a
drop
of water
now
blot
it,
try
scratching
on the left.
Clumsy
can't you
leave the
paper
here and
there? Did
you ever
think of
going to
Venice?

D. Levine 64

JOHN RUSKIN

LEWIS CARROLL

EDWARD LEAR

BEATRIX POTTER

113

RUDYARD KIPLING

BENJAMIN DISRAELI

(with Queen Victoria)

THOMAS HARDY

AUBREY BEARDSLEY

OSCAR WILDE

GEORGE BERNARD SHAW

JOSEPH CONRAD

RUPERT BROOKE

MAX BEERBOHM

FORD MADOX FORD

ARNOLD BENNETT

Somerset Maugham

E. M. Forster

H. G. Wells

123

SIDNEY AND BEATRICE WEBB

BERTRAND RUSSELL

125

WILLIAM BUTLER YEATS

126

W. B. Yeats, D. H. Lawrence, Wyndham Lewis,

T. S. Eliot, Ezra Pound

LEONARD WOOLF

VIRGINIA WOOLF

LYTTON STRACHEY

JAMES JOYCE

JAMES JOYCE

Robert Graves

Evelyn Waugh

D. H. LAWRENCE

SEAN O'CASEY

JOHN MAYNARD KEYNES

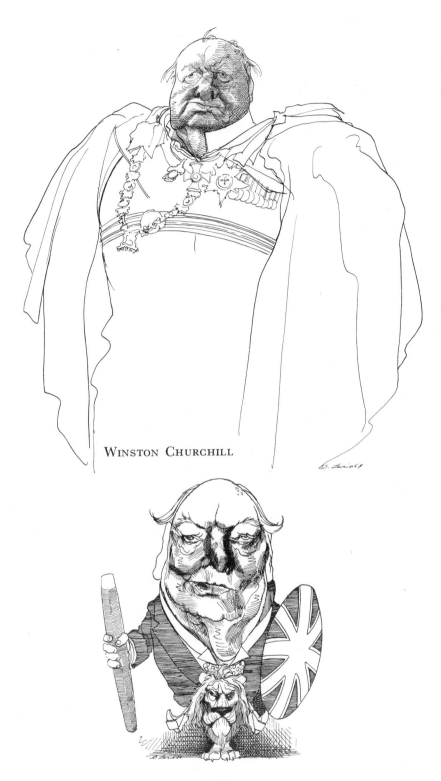

WINSTON CHURCHILL

J. R. R. TOLKIEN

Arnold Toynbee

H. R. Trevor-Roper

137

GRAHAM GREENE

Dame Edith Sitwell

Doris Lessing

C. P. Snow

LAWRENCE DURRELL

WILLIAM GOLDING

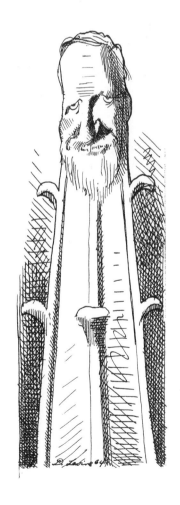

Angus Wilson

Brendan Behan

ANTHONY POWELL

NOEL COWARD

DYLAN THOMAS

144

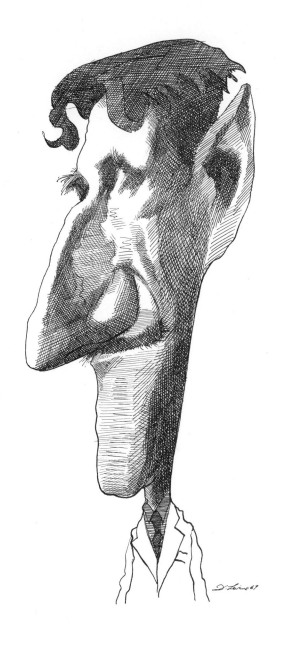

GEORGE ORWELL

145

TWIGGY

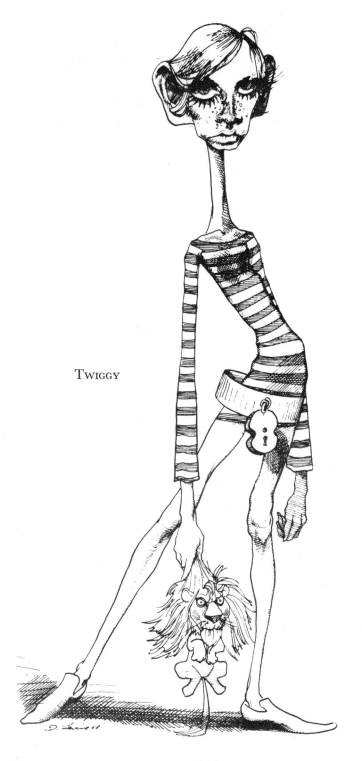

THE BEATLES

INDEX